W9-CCZ-828

GREAT AMERICAN GARDENS

A Photographic Celebration

STACEY LYNN McNUTT

First published in the United States of America in 1999 by Courage Books.

9 8 7 6 5 4 3 2 1
Digit on the right indicates the number of this printing.

Library of Congress Cataloging-in-Publication Number 98-72526

ISBN 0-7624-0421-3

This book was designed and produced by
TODTRI Book Publishers
P. O. Box 572, New York, NY 10116-0572
Fax: (212) 695-6984
e-mail: todtri@mindspring.com

Author: Stacey Lynn McNutt

Publisher: Robert M. Tod
Senior Editor: Edward Douglas
Designer: Mark Weinberg
Typesetting: Command-O, NYC

Printed and bound in Singapore

Published by Courage Books, an imprint of
Running Press Book Publishers
125 South Twenty-second Street
Philadelphia, PA 19103-4399

Visit us on the web!
www.runningpress.com

PICTURE CREDITS

Gene Ahrens 7, 8–9, 16 (top & bottom), 17, 19, 22, 23, 26, 27, 34, 60, 70

Patti McConville & Les Sumner 12, 18, 20, 40–41, 42, 43 (top), 45, 49 (right)

Picture Perfect 69
William D. Adams 75 (top)
Kit Breen 52(top)
Cecile Brunswick 56–57
William B. Folsom 46
Mark E, Gibson 50 (top), 51 (top), 53 (bottom), 54, 58 (top & bottom)
Bob Higbee 59
Michael J. Howell 53 (top)
Arnold John Kaplan 51 (bottom)
Stephen Kirkpatrick 49 (left)
Jose Raga 77
John Warden (52 (bottom)
David F. Wisse 35

Lee Snider/Photo Images 4, 5, 6, 10, 11, 13, 14, 15, 21 (top & bottom), 24–25, 28, 29, 30, 31, 32 (top & bottom), 33 (top & bottom), 36, 37, 38, 39 (top & bottom), 43 (bottom), 44, 47, 48, 50 (bottom), 55 (top & bottom), 61, 62, 63, 64 (top & bottom), 65, 66, 67 (top & bottom), 68 (top & bottom), 71 (top & bottom), 72–73, 74, 75 (bottom), 76, 78 (top & bottom), 79

CONTENTS

INTRODUCTION

Gardens provide us with an intimate look at a region's history. Though the first American gardens were necessarily simple, even those simple plots could be statements of what the first colonists believed America could be. At the time, they visualized a nation of small landholders.

It was not a country of cleared and enclosed farmlands ruled over by landed aristocrats who built elaborate artificial landscape gardens on their country estates. It was instead a vast wilderness. Reports of the country's abundant flora and fauna, and descriptions of friendly Indians convinced English and Dutch colonists that they were traveling to paradise. The Spanish, who sent explorers into the North America South and Southwest in search of gold, believed it was not.

The story of the American garden goes hand-in-hand with the history of American itself. The American garden owes its diversity not just to the

RIGHT: This house, built in 1739 as a mission to convert local Indians to Christianity, would have had a simple garden at best. This twentieth century restoration attempts to recreate the informality of colonial domestic planting. _Stockbridge, Massachusetts._

OPPOSITE: Middleton Place, a former rice plantation, is noted for its landscaped garden which is perhaps the oldest in America. Begun around 1741, the contruction of its terraces and canals required one hundred slaves and ten years to complete. _Charleston, South Carolina._

variations in the vast and changing countryside and climate, but also to a variety of period styles and cultures. Philosophy influenced the development of the American garden almost as much as the soil, site and climate.

The first American gardens were not so much what the new country was, but what the environment was not. A formal colonial garden was governed by order. It created civilization on the edge of the wilderness, much like the courtyard water gardens of the Persians made a cool fragrant oasis in the desert.

Gardens are, of course, much more than what the world is not. They are living affirmation that the seasons pass and life goes on. In this way, gardens make themselves more than a quiet refuge and a place of contemplation. Gardens become a place of comfort and companionship. Gardening itself despite the practical hard work, keeps gardeners not very far from wonder, and makes gardening a process that is as mysterious as the spring leaf or blossom on a dry twig.

The American garden is also a place of discovery. From the time of the arrival of the first colonists, botanists and horticulturists recorded and collected native American trees, plants and flowers. Unlike the Spanish,

BELOW: The Elizabethan Gardens are a twentieth century homage to Queen Elizabeth I and the Lost Colony. With formal plantings and statuary, they resemble more the aristocratic gardens of sixteenth-century Tudor England than anything that could be seen in the New World at the time. *Roanoke Island, North Carolina*

LEFT: **Completed in 1770, Tryon Palace was once the state house of North Carolina. Shortly after the Revolution it burned to the ground, but was reconstructed in the 1950s. Its gounds and gardens reflect the eighteenth-century formality appropriate to a royal governor.** ***New Bern, North Carolina.***

English and Dutch explorers saw untold wealth in the abundant plants, flowers, herbs, and trees of North America. In the early seventeenth century, enterprising entrepreneurs established a thriving trade in plants. They were instrumental in filling the English country estate gardens with North American species and in sending European plants across the Atlantic to grace the gardens of American colonists.

As the gardens of the New World developed in size, variety, and design, the theme of these new gardens became the prevailing theme of all garden styles—formal, picturesque, or wild. That theme is unity. Unity between house and garden, and harmony between man and his environment. Any gardener will tell you is that this is a difficult balance to strike, but achieving it even temporarily is something like perfection.

American Gardens *traces the influences upon garden design; the histories of particular gardens; and the inspirations that lead to innovations in garden design. Whether it is the restored gardens of Mount Vernon or the small garden of a city townhouse, our enjoyment of these places springs from experiencing the most intimate spirit of American history.*

FOLLOWING PAGE: **The Azalea Woods of the Winterthur Gardens perfectly exemplfy the English landscape style in the way they fully exploit the natural beauty of the Brandywine Valley.** ***Wilmington, Delaware.***

CHAPTER ONE

GARDENS OF COLONIAL AMERICA AND THE OLD SOUTH

The English and Dutch pilgrims who settled North America's eastern seaboard and the shores of American's eastern rivers believed they were traveling to a wild paradise where vegetation grew in such abundance that it needed little cultivation. Gardens were of the first importance to the pilgrims who brought their own garden traditions to the new world with packets of seeds and roots.

LEFT: **Herbs have many uses and are important in preparing foods, cosmetics, and medicines. However, for the stern Puritans the only possible use for these plants were as medications to relieve a variety of ailments.** ***Haddam, Connecticut.***

EARLY COLONIAL GARDENS

For the early settlers, a garden was a cleared area where medicinal herbs and vegetables were grown. A simple timber fence or thorny hedge protected it from animals and the encroaching wilderness. Vegetables and herbs were usually interplanted in rectangular plots located at the front or side of the house that enjoyed the most sun.

Gardens with paths and flower beds were not a part of early colonial life. Pleasure gardens were the property of affluent monarchs and aristocrats, not humble pilgrims, and flowers though things of beauty were a symbol of the transience of earthly pleasures. These first settlers were primarily concerned with the back-breaking work of clearing land and building communities. Plants were grown because they were useful.

We have few maps of early colonial and Native American gardens. However, the Pilgrims corresponded frequently with English botanists. These records indicate that the herb garden was an ample one, and just as important as the kitchen garden. The frequent correspondence on medicinal herbs, established an early pharmacological trade that proved essential to the health of the colonists.

COLONIAL HERB GARDENS

Herbs such as marigolds, hyssop, feverfew, tansy, and gilly flowers were planted out in log bordered beds with American herbs such as bergamot—which was brewed to make Oswega tea—sweet joe pye, and American sweet cicely.

The hardy sages were the most commonly grown herbs in the colonial garden. The pilgrims used sage for seasoning, as a tea, and as a remedy for a number of ailments. Tradition has it that sage was valued so highly, it was dried and taken to China where it was exchanged pound for pound for tea.

Mint was a common remedy for indigestion and native mints and pennyroyal were ubiquitous in the colonial garden. Colonists in the south used

OPPOSITE: **This bed of tulips mixed with pansies brings to mind the Dutch, who were the first settlers to plant small formal gardens in the New World. Even after New Amsterdam became New York, Dutch gardening skills, ideas, and designs were widely imitated throughout the colonies.** ***New Bern, North Carolina***

ABOVE: **Here is an eighteenth-century formal garden typical of the colonial period. Geometrically shaped beds filled with a variety of flowers and decorative plants are surrounded by straight gravel walkways. The charming topiaries provide a vertical accent to the low horizontal design.** ***Philadelphia, Pennsylvania.***

mint as fresh garnishes for summer drinks and dishes. Fennel was grown for its leaves and seeds, and was eaten to relieve hunger pangs on days of fasting.

DUTCH COLONIAL GARDENS

Dutch immigrants to the New Netherlands—later renamed New York by the English—were better supplied and prepared for settlement, than their English neighbors. The Dutch government supplied them with farm animals and equipped them to begin cultivation of their rugged, fertile plots. Dutch farms and orchards in Manhattan, Long Island, and the Hudson River Valley flourished.

The Dutch were expert farmers and, unlike the Puritans, they were lovers of flowers. They were rightfully considered Europe's finest gardeners; and were the first colonists to plant small formal gardens. The Castello Map of New Amsterdam (1660) shows these gardens on the southernmost tip of Manhattan.

Nearly every house has a small, geometrical, formal garden in the restrained Dutch style. The map may have exaggerated the actual number of gardens, but not the style, which imitated in miniature the Palace Gardens at Het-Loo. Topiary was substituted for statuary, and the balanced design was based on a central axis.

The Dutch garden was the essence of formal simplicity. In the mid-seventeenth century, when the English colonists moved from subsistence to success, they began to make pleasure gardens as well. The English imitated the Dutch garden plan "of the gentry" that emphasized symmetry with walls, hedges, decorative, low, knot gardens and small, trimmed trees.

In 1629, a special class of Dutch settlers was encouraged to emigrate to the New Netherlands. These immigrants were given land grants of sixteen miles along one side of "any navigable river" or of eight miles on facing shores on the condition that the land would be colonized by at least fifty people. These grants along the Hudson River established the future country estates of New York's landed aristocracy.

PHILADELPHIA'S QUAKER GARDENS

Pennsylvania was colonized slightly later than most of the other colonies, but it quickly became the center of American horticulture. More than one garden historian credits the Quakers for giving Philadelphia this prominence. Botany and the natural sciences were acceptable pleasurable vocations to the Quakers who eschewed the arts and entertainments. Botany had the added value of being helpful to the community.

John Bartram was one of Philadelphia's prominent Quakers, and was recognized by the Swedish natural scientist, Carolus Linneaus, as "the greatest natural botanist in the world." On land owned by the Quakers of Philadelphia, he created a botanic garden devoted to the cultivation of a wide variety of plants.From his botanic garden, Bartram sent nearly one hundred and fifty different plants and seeds to Britain, enriching the English garden with many native American plants. His correspondence with the English botanist Peter Collinson forms the basis of an incredible record of indigenous species found in the colonies. His work was continued by his son, William, whose successful plant exploration expeditions surpassed his father's contributions.

LEMON HILL

The most elegant of Philadelphia's gardens were found on the hillside estates above the Schuylkill River. Lemon Hill was among these estates, and was designed in the English landscape style. It

LEFT: **The gardens of Lemon Hill, a mansion dating from the Federal period, were laid out in the English landscape style. This property is one of a group of seven open to the public and known as the Fairmount Park Mansions. *Philadelphia, Pennsylvania.***

BELOW: **The garden of Carlyle House, which dates from 1753, is located in the rear of the mansion. Artfully arranged evergreen trees and shrubbery make this a pleasant and private retreat at any time of the year. *Alexandria, Virginia.***

enjoyed a southern exposure on which its conservatories were situated. This made its hothouses perfect for lemons, oranges and pineapples. First called, The Hills, the house was burned down during the Revolutionary War. The gardens were subsequently restored and the house rebuilt, and renamed Lemon Hill.

Lemon Hill shared its pleasant aspect on the river with an equally famous estate called, "Pleasant Hill," once owned by Benedict Arnold. The house and garden have been restored based on old records and descriptions, and are now open to the public. They are situated in Fairmount Park, Philadelphia's 4,500 acre city park.

OPPOSITE: **The Nemours Estate was built by Alfred I. Du Pont, scion of one of America's oldest industrial families. The statue shown here is the focal point of the estate's maze garden. *Wilmington, Delaware.***

NORTH VS SOUTH

Colonial America was settled by small farmers. Initially, both north and south were agrarian economies. By 1775, New Jersey was so well planted with orchards that it was said to surpass anything in England. Maryland had its share of plantations, as did Pennsylvania's Brandywine Valley and Connecticut.

Country estates were not the exclusive realm of gentleman farmers. Many acres of Delaware's section of the Brandywine Valley were acquired by the Nemours Du Pont family in 1800. Originally manufacturers of gunpowder, the Du Ponts established America's first great industrial fortune.

The Du Ponts and their descendants built impressive country estates in the Brandywine Valley. Today, three are open to the public. The Nemours Mansion and Gardens has formal French gardens. The famous Winterthur Gardens are designed in the English landscape style. The grounds of the Hagley Museum cover two hundred and thirty acres and includes the original family home.

Wherever—and as soon as—colonists had means to build a garden, and beautify their surroundings they did so. Bostonians were not unique in their displays of civic pride. Georgetown, originally part of Virginia, was a profitable tobacco port. Its early prosperity can be seen in its Georgian architecture and equally fine gardens.

THE VIRGINIA COLONY

From the establishment of Jamestown to the outbreak of the Civil War, America subsisted almost wholly on its agriculture. Tobacco was the main crop of the Virginia colony. Between 1612 and 1699, profits from the colony's tobacco plantations enriched a number of farmers to the degree that they could devote themselves to the gentlemanly task of planning and planting the civic and private pleasure gardens, of the Virginia colony's new capital, Williamsburg.

RIGHT: **The garden at the back of this Colonial Williamsburg house is divided into two distinct areas. In this way, the charming flower-lined walk in the foreground offers an area for relaxation that is separated from the more mundane activities associated with the house and its kitchen. *Colonial Williamsburg, Virginia.***

RIGHT: **The gardens of the Governor's Palace in Colonial Williamsburg, like the house itself, have been restored to the way they appeared in 1770. The spacious overall design seen here complements the Georgian-style architecture of the palace. *Colonial Williamsburg, Virginia.***

Colonial Williamsburg was settled on a ridge midway between the James and the York Rivers. It had a good situation in aspect, climate, and soil. Begun in 1713, the town's gardens were planted and laid out to display the best and most fashionable of English garden designs.

The Williamsburg that can be visited today is a twentieth century recreation of the original gardens. The expense of the extensive restoration was funded by John D. Rockefeller, Jr., and the restoration itself was based on records found in the Bodleian library in England.

The original grounds of the governor's palace covered three hundred and seventy acres. The Governor's palace, arguably the finest dwelling in the colonies, was built to serve as a symbol of royal authority. The cost of construction was subsidized by a new tax on the purchase of individual slaves.

Besides the ornamental plantings, there was an orchard and a kitchen garden. The grounds were bordered by linden trees that were imported from Scotland. The symmetry of the walks and flower beds owes much to the balanced proportions of Georgian architecture. At the same time, the garden's spaciousness was a distinctive element of the ornamental gardens of Virginia plantations.

The town was planned by Sir Francis Nicholson, Governor from 1698 to 1705. Originally each town lot was a uniform half acre, and was set back exactly six feet from the street. In the back of every house, was a garden—as visitors to Williamsburg today can see. The flower gardens were usually made of beds divided by crossing walks, whether the garden was based on an oval, circle, rectangle or a square. Lawns were not a feature of these small, compact gardens. The emphasis instead is on the colors and patterns of the flower beds; and the trees. Deciduous native species provided gardens with dappled light and shade.

By the time the English colonies declared their independence in 1776, there were many beautiful plantation gardens throughout Virginia, up the rivers of Old Dominion and on the coast and the rivers of the Carolinas. However, two gardens surpassed all the rest in their aspect and individual treatment of plants and use of design. It is through the diaries and letters of the two men who established Mount Vernon and Monticello that we have a complete history of these gardens. The two men were George Washington and Thomas Jefferson.

ABOVE: As citizens of the capital of a thriving colony, the people of Williamsburg made their houses as attractive as possible by imitating the latest gardening trends in eighteenth-century England. _Colonial Williamsburg, Virginia._

MOUNT VERNON

Mount Vernon is located in North Virginia in an area that was and is popular for its beauty, fertility, and proximity to Washington, D.C. Aside from its historic importance, this estate is famous for its formal gardens and collection of rare old-fashioned roses.

Mount Vernon was established in 1754, and was built from Washington's own plans. His ideas on garden design were influenced by the prevailing ideas in eighteenth century England, which favored a natural landscape style over the strictly formal, symmetrical designs of previous centuries.

A book on garden planning by Batty Langley, published in 1728, was particularly influential. Langley eschewed the use of formal topiary and parterres. Instead, he advised planting thickets of trees and shrubs that would be allowed to mature, then ornamentals and exotics could be naturalized within the shelter of the created "wilderness."

One of the notable features of the English landscape garden was the ha-ha. This was a ditch with concealed sides that kept grazing cattle and sheep at a scenic distance from the house, which at Mount Vernon has a sweeping view of the Potomac River. The ditch was dubbed ha-ha, because walkers exclaimed, "ha!" when they came upon them to prevent their companions from stumbling into it.

When Washington could not be at Mount Vernon, his nephew advised him on the development of the garden. Letters between the two show that Washington wanted Mount Vernon to be styled in the new tradition of the ornamental landscape garden with sweeping lawns on both fronts of the house, formal areas on either side of the bowling green, and "groves, shrubberies and wildernesses" bordering the serpentine drives. Visitors to Mount Vernon admired the incorporation of pleasure and kitchen gardens, and Washington's broad knowledge of plant materials, and fine sense of design. Mount Vernon continues to define the pastoral American garden in which the artificial order of the garden appears to blend naturally with the surrounding landscape.

MONTICELLO

In 1768, Thomas Jefferson realized his boyhood dream of building a home on top of a forested hill. Unlike Washington, Jefferson spent a number of years abroad. Being an avid gardener and natural scientist, Jefferson took every opportunity to see the gardens of France, Germany, and Italy. He even spent one spring touring a number of English estates, including the landscape parks of Stowe, Chiswick, and Blenheim. For all he learned in these places, Jefferson recognized that the English style could not be successfully imported to Virginia because of the differences in climate. The intense sunlight of the South demanded more tress for shade and fewer open spaces.

BELOW: Though Washington preferred the English landscape style in his plans for the grounds of Mount Vernon, some areas, like this intimate pleasure garden, included formal elements such as topiary. *Mount Vernon, Virginia.*

Jefferson brought not only his avid interest in botany and horticulture to Monticello, but also a republican vision to garden design. The landscape and the house were intended to exemplify the heights of classical thought and design in the wilderness of the New World. Jefferson's detailed notebooks show the observation of a born naturalist and the precision of an economy expert. Monticello was a sort of philosophical and botanical laboratory.

It is clear from his letters that Jefferson loved trees. When these began to mature in the middle of his second presidential term, Jefferson began

OPPOSITE: The building of Monticello was a lifelong project for Thomas Jefferson, who never stopped devising additions and improvements. He lavished similar attention on the grounds, carefully choosing plants and colored blooms to line the many flowered walkways. *Monticello, Virginia.*

work on Monticello's distinctive flower beds. The flower bordered walk at Monticello was designed without hedges of dwarf box, which were a common feature of Dutch and colonial formal flower gardens. The oval and circular beds in the lawns adjoining the house were planted with red flowers that bloomed throughout the spring, summer and fall. Jefferson also designed the grounds at the University of Virginia. These were begun in 1817, and later restored over a three year period in the late 1940s. Among the features at the University of Virginia are serpentine walls. These were sometimes used in English kitchen gardens to protect fruit trees esplaniered against them, and were generally planted from east to west to best reflect the sunlight.

ABOVE: **Jefferson was a keen gardener and constantly experimented with new species and varieties of plants. He was as interested in the vegetables and herbs in his kitchen garden as he was with flowering and ornamental plants.** ***Monticello, Virginia.***

SOUTH CAROLINA'S COLONIAL ESTATES

Charleston is city of many gardens. Many private arbors and brick edged flower beds can be glimpsed through the wrought iron front gates. Modern-day Charleston is one of the best-preserved cities of the Old South. Restoration of fine homes and gardens is a matter of civic pride, and residents over three centuries have learned to rebuild. The city has suffered epidemics, earthquakes, hurricanes, and fires.

Rice was the cash crop of the South Carolina's riverside plantations. It was a labor-intensive crop. Cultivation of rice began around Charleston at the end of the seventeenth century. Initially it was farmed in inland swamps, but enormous plantations were created with land grants from the English Crown. Planters then used the marshes along the Carolinas' tidal rivers. Middleton Place and Cypress Gardens are among the largest and oldest of these plantations.

RICE PLANTATIONS

In 1740, Henry Middleton began landscaping Middleton Place with the graduated, sculpted terraces that make up the slope down to the river and end in two water basins. The rural park of Middleton Place united a working plantation with an ornamental landscape garden. The design was based firmly in French garden tradition of a central radial axis. The original garden which has been largely restored included a flower garden and a bowling green. To complete it took nine years and the work of one hundred slaves, who would also have been essential to the cultivation of rice, which is a labor intensive crop.

Much of the garden has been restored, including an alley of camellias that leads to the seven hundred-foot-long reflecting canal. Tradition has it that the French botanist and gardener Andre Michaux introduced camellias and azaleas to Middleton Place in 1783. Native magnolias

LEFT: Azaleas are a special feature of Charleston gardens. This antebellum mansion, with its wrought-iron gate, is typical of many houses throughout this historic city. Abundant sunlight and a long growing season make it a gardener's paradise. *Charleston, South Carolina.*

LEFT: The gardens of South Carolina's Magnolia Plantation were begun in the 1680s. Though the plantation house was destroyed in the Civil War, the gardens survived and are today a mecca for tourists who enjoy their lush plantings. *Charleston, South Carolina.*

help to give Middleton Place much of its indigenous character.

In the eighteenth century, Cypress Gardens was a rice plantation called Deam Hall. The rice fields of Deam Hall reverted to marshes after the Civil War. The original estate was designed much like a formal European garden, but used native plants such as magnolia and live oaks for shade. The Cypress Gardens can now be visited by boat, and has been underplanted with beds of azaleas whose vibrant hues contrast with the dark water and the snaking roots of the cypress trees.

Georgia had its rice plantations, too, along the Savannah and Big and Little Ogeechee Rivers. These rivaled those of South Carolina in their beauty. Live Oaks grew especially well along the Savannah, and the graceful avenues of these oaks became a symbol for the southern plantation.

SOUTHERN TOWN GARDENS

Savannah was settled in 1733, and its charming town gardens were allotted in its city plan. Larger plots allowed for a small formal garden, planted in the intricate geometric style that was typical of

BELOW: **Many old Savannah houses have small front gardens protected by wrought-iron enclosures. Typcally, these houses also have a much more extensive and elaborate garden area at the rear of the house. *Savannah, Georgia.***

LEFT: **Savannah is noted as a city of beautiful, flower-filled squares that are surrounded on all four sides by stately mansions dating far back into the city's history. Here a portion of Monterey Square is seen. *Savannah, Georgia.***

eighteenth century gardens. Beds were edged with bricks or tiles or with clipped box. Plantings became more open when larger flowering shrubs such as camellias, oleanders, and azaleas became popular.

These front gardens were enclosed by a wrought-iron fence. Very small front gardens were usually enclosed by brick, but even these had climbing roses or a small fruit tree. Back gardens were more spacious and were surrounded with brick walls that enclosed flowering shrubs, citrus and fig trees, and usually an herb garden. Grape and rose covered arbors were common.

PLANTATIONS OF THE DEEP SOUTH

Before 1815, the only main difference between the northern and southern colonies was the climate. The southern climate offered one long growing season broken only by a few months of winter. This climate is inhospitable to plants that require a period of dormancy, such as peonies, to blossom, seed, and blossom again. But it is a garden paradise for tender plants.

The invention of the cotton gin in 1793 enabled farmers to process great quantities of cotton quickly. Because of this, together with the mechanization of the textile industry in England, cotton surpassed wool as the most popular cloth. In the South cotton became "king." and cotton plantations expanded beyond South Carolina and Georgia as far west as Texas.

Gardening quickly became the favorite recreation of wealthy planters and merchants. The Nashville and Cumberland regions of Tennessee were full of beautiful estates including the homes of three United States Presidents: Andrew Johnson, James K. Polk, and Andrew Jackson.

Polk Place is notable for the bluegrass lawn that surrounds the house. Andrew Jackson's "Hermitage," with plantings supervised by Jackson himself, constitutes an arboretum of the trees of middle Tennessee.

FOLLOWING PAGE: **The restored gardens of the William Paca house retain many elements of their original design, including an eighteenth-century summer house and a Chineses Chippendale bridge. *Annapolis, Maryland.***

ABOVE: **One of the most lavish and stately Southern mansions is Stanton Hall, built in 1858 just prior to the Civil War. Its grounds are ample and spacious to match the palatial proportions of the house itself. *Natchez, Mississippi.***

Many travelers to the South commented on the long hedges of roses, which were first used as fencing on some plantations. Roses with cypresses, live oaks, crepe-myrtle, magnolias, oleanders and azaleas became a feature of southern gardens. Among the Mississippi and Louisiana cotton and sugar plantations, those in Natchez were among the wealthiest and were thought to be among the finest.

FRENCH INFLUENCE

The French settled in the South on the Gulf of Mexico at Fort Conde (now Mobile, Alabama) and in New Orleans. They also established two significant ports on the Mississippi River, Layfayette and Baton Rouge. So it is no surprise to find gardens that imitated the formal French style in the deep South, especially in cities and plantations near the Gulf and along the Mississippi River.

New Orleans was acquired by the United States in 1803 as part of the Louisiana Purchase. The Old Ursuline Convent, erected in 1749 by order of Louis XV, is the only building that remains of the original colony. Nevertheless, New Orleans is remarkably well-preserved, and its blend of French and Spanish architecture and garden design can be seen in the city's courtyard gardens.

These courtyards gardens are in the Mediterranean tradition—luxurious enclosures that shelter fruits, flowers, and a large shade tree. Vine-covered galleries also protect the house and inhabitants from the sun. Filigreed iron work allows passers-by to glimpse the interior of the courtyards, while abundant blossoms and creeping vines preserved privacy.

BELOW: **The first mistress of Rosedown Plantation, Martha Turnbull, was a devoted horticulturalist and designed every aspect of this 30-acre garden. Here a wide variety of flowers were planted in formal boxwood enclosures, including some of the first Oriental species to be grown in this region. *Feliciana, Louisiana.***

SOUTHERN SPANISH GARDENS

The Spanish settled Florida and parts of Georgia. They took full advantage of Florida's tropical climate, introducing many European shade trees and ornamental flowers, as well as the cultivation of citrus fruits.

St. Augustine was the Spanish stronghold in Florida. Built on a wooded hill, the city was Spain itself. Figs, limes, oranges, and grapes were cultivated in orchards and in private gardens. Shade trees lined the city's streets, and a wide plaza took the place of a village green. The balconies of the stone houses were draped with flowers and vines. The porticos that served as entryways to the houses were covered with vines or sheltered behind shrubs.

French, Spanish, and English styles in garden design co-mingled in the gracious estates and city gardens of the South until just before the Civil War. The temperate climate of the region allowed a wide range of tender and exotic plants to flourish—hibiscus, verbena, poinsettias, and, in some places, orchids. However, the lavishness of the South's ante-bellum gardens was eventually surpassed when greater fortunes were made during the Gilded Age. These newly rich individuals built homes and gardens throughout the country that were equal to their elevated social and financial standing.

BELOW: The European-style formal garden of the Ringling Museum is a perfect setting for the display of the museum's collection of classical and Renaissance statuary. *Sarasota, Florida.*

LEFT: The cloister of a twelfth-century Spanish monastery was dismantled and shipped to the United States by William Randolph Hearst. Eventually, it was reassembled near Miami and today provides a cool retreat for the contemplative visitor. *North Miami, Florida.*

CHAPTER TWO

PLEASURE GARDENS NEW

To the early settlers, the seasons in New England declared themselves dramatically. The colorful fall foliage made colonists value the display of the deciduous trees as much as the perennial verdure of evergreens. The vividness of the fall leaves somehow compensated for the death of summer blossoms.

Fall foliage is especially beautiful in Vermont and New Hampshire, states which were still on the frontier in the eighteenth century. Though small, settlements in these places were not without their garden traditions. Most towns were established around a village green. Houses with front flower gardens or forecourts, were common by mid-century.

Records show that there were as many as a hundred country-seats in late colonial New England in which there were fine houses set in landscapes of excellent design. Noteworthy estates could be found throughout the region, and on many of them could be seen a plant not indigenous to North America. This was the purple lilac which had been brought across the Atlantic by many travelers and had established itself as a popular garden shrub by the 1730s. Eventually, this native of eastern Europe and possibly Asia, became the state flower of New Hampshire.

PLEASURE GARDENS NEW

Boston can lay claim to being one of America's oldest cities. Massachusetts assumed the mayflower as the state flower—lest there be any doubters. Civic pride has always run high, and Boston was proud of its gardens from its earliest days.

Two of the most notable of the pre-Revolutionary War gardens were located on Beacon Hill. One belonged to Thomas Hancock, the uncle of John Hancock, who cultivated dwarf and espaniered fruit trees, as well as garden topiary shaped from yew. The other was the creation of a French Huguenot, Andrew Faneuil.

The Faneuil house was situated behind a terraced flower garden and commanded a view of the Boston Common. His grounds were notable for having the first greenhouse in Boston, and for their extravagant garden architecture, including wrought-iron railings, topped with golden balls, and a pagoda-like summerhouse with a gilded grasshopper vane.

These imposing Boston gardens were the precursors of the many fine gardens that would grace Massachusetts in the late eighteenth and early nineteenth centuries.

GORE PLACE

Shortly after 1800, an outstanding estate was created in Waltham, Massachusetts. It became known

BELOW: The John Quincy Adams House, with its borders of flowers and stretches of lawn, remains much as it was when it was the home of two presidents and two generations of their descendents. *Quincy, Massachusetts.*

OPPOSITE: The Codman House, built in the 1740s, has been improved and embellished by successive generations. Today both the house and its 16-acre landscaped grounds stand as fine examples of eighteenth- and nineteenth-century style. *Lincoln, Massachusetts.*

ABOVE: The restored colonial gardens of the seventeenth-century House of the Seven Gables are a modern-day attempt to recreate some of the formal elements that influenced early American garden design. *Salem, Massachusetts*

RIGHT: The north front of Boscobel, built in 1804, is enhanced by rows of deciduous trees and evergreen shrubs. These lines of upward reaching and ground clinging greenery become even for dramatic in the autumn when the trees are ablaze with color. *Garrison, New York.*

LEFT: **In the past, kitchen gardens that produced a quantity of vegetables and herbs for most of the year were a necessity. However, the great estates of the well-to-do had the means and the space to grow luscious fruits as well. Here we see the orangerie at Boscobel. *Garrison, New York.***

BELOW: **The simplicity of two lines of colorful zinnias is all that is needed to entice us to enter the dark and plain Buckingham House, built in 1671. *Old Saybrook, Connecticut.***

BELOW: **Portsmouth, as New Hampshire's earliest center of prosperity, has a rich gardening history stretching from the seventeenth century to the early 1900s. Forty-two historic homes have survived the vagaries of time. Shown here is the lovely Prescott Garden. *Portsmouth, New Hampshire.***

as Gore Place, and its style marks an important turn in garden design.

Gore Place overlooks large expanses of lawns, hills, a wide variety of forest trees, and the Charles River. Like the English landscape styles that had inspired the gardens of Washington and Jefferson, the gardens of Gore Place were shaped into an English-style park.

Christopher Gore had traveled to London in 1796 as a representative of the United States government. During his stay, Gore enjoyed visiting English country estates, and was especially taken with those designed in the picturesque style.

This new philosophy of gardening sought not to impose order on nature, but to express the nature of the place itself. Formality was banished, and gardens were designed to evoke paintings of nature and contemplative states of mind. The resulting semi-wildness of the picturesque garden seemed ideal for the gardens of New England.

After Gore returned home in 1805, he spent the next twenty-two years sculpting his garden, and creating naturalistic scenes that included

water, fields, and artfully placed trees. Romanticism, a belief in the perfection of nature, had arrived in the American garden. It reigned where formality and reason had asserted themselves earlier. Romanticism complimented the American love of the rural ideal. This love of the pastoral lingered in American literature and gardens as the United States expanded and industry transformed urban areas and formerly wild stretches of country.

The Romantics believed that there was more than one truth. The Romantic philosophy recognized the value of variety, and this recognition came to be of infinite importance to American garden design, where innovations developed from the belief that there is more than one way to make a garden.

BY NATURE INSPIRED

By the 1830s, the New England Transcendentalists articulated this new vision with their delight in nature and the natural world, partly in response to the rapid, uncontrolled urban growth. They asked for a new appreciation of nature, and demanded a new urban aesthetic. It arrived in 1831.

Mount Auburn in Cambridge, Massachusetts was the first landscaped public cemetery. Before its establishment, cemeteries were grim places of burial, developed only because small churchyards, the traditional site of burial, could not accommodate more graves.

Mount Auburn was designed as a naturalist landscape park. It was described as an "open cemetery"

ABOVE: **Cambridge, Massachusetts made a major contribution to American garden and park design with the creation of a cemetery known as Mount Auburn. It was a naturalistic landscape park, open and serene, that was imitated across the United States.** ***Lehigh County, Pennsylvania.***

ABOVE: **Boston Common is the oldest public park in the eastern United States. Adjacent to it are the Public Gardens, a relatively small area that includes expansive lawns, tree-shaded walkways, and a small lake.** ***Boston, Massachusetts.***

because railing and hedging around the graves themselves was not permitted. With the uniform beauty of the cemetery in mind, monuments, markers and plantings of trees and shrubs were regulated. The atmosphere was one of peaceful reflection.

Other American cities quickly followed Boston's example and designed cemeteries to rival Mount Auburn, notably Cincinnati, Philadelphia, and Rochester, New York. Visitors to Philadelphia's Laurel Hill Cemetery totaled thirty thousand between the months of April and December of 1848. The popularity of the cemeteries showed civic minded citizens the general desire for public parks.

PUBLIC GARDENS

The rural cemetery movement gained momentum during the nineteenth century. Woodland sites were landscaped and maintained by professional designers and gardeners as burial places, and they became increasingly popular.

At this same time, landscape gardener Andrew Jackson Downing began to draw America's attention to the "special mission" of the new European public parks, believing in their ability to promote "a fraternal spirit" among people. In 1843, Downing reprinted in his journal *The Horticulturist* an account of a visit to England's first public park, Birkenhead. The writer was a young man by the name of Frederick Law Olmsted, who would become the forefather of landscape architecture in America.

OPPOSITE: **Statuary and monuments are frequently used to add interest to landscape design. In this small park from the nineteenth century, an exuberantly decorated memorial urn is surround by a colorful grouping of gerraniums, coleus, and cannas.** ***Saratoga_Springs, New York.***

The publication prompted a meeting between the two men, and provided Olmsted with his first introduction to Downing's partner, the English architect, Calvert Vaux. Together Vaux and Downing were designing a public park for Washington, D.C. that would run from the Capitol to the White House. After Downing's premature death, Olmsted and Vaux became partners.

In 1858, they submitted the design that became New York's Central Park. Olmsted designed many more public parks and private gardens, and helped to make public parks the gothic cathedrals of America's major cities. Out of the landfill of Boston's Harbor, he created the reed bound pools, flower gardens, and meadows of the Back Bay Fens. The accomplishment of Central Park earned Olmsted an appointment as chairman of the committee governing the public use of Yosemite National Park, where he worked to make necessary roads and trails, and situated lodgings as unobtrusively as possible.

PRIVATE GARDENS

As the frontier expanded westward and the continent was explored and settled, the American garden did not shrink in importance. To the contrary, as the nation moved outward, Americans, as individuals, were turning inward, cultivating their own gardens in greater numbers. If America was vast, the private garden was comfortingly small by comparison.

Private gardens, especially small city gardens, became a pastoral refuge in an increasingly industrialized world. Gardening never ceased to be a pleasure, and the nineteenth century was a time of invention and horticultural innovation. The invention of the lawn mower in the 1850s affected garden design, and made the lawn a large important garden feature. Flowers and their colors had the most immediate effect upon large and small gardens.

ABOVE: Bodies of water were effectively used by Frederick Law Olmstead and Calvert Vaux in their designs for parks, to provide contrast and enhance the feeling of rural serenity in the heart of great a city. As an added bonus, they also attracted wildlife. The bridge seen here crosses a small lake in Prospect Park. *Brooklyn, New York.*

RIGHT: Daffodils are a special springtime feature in many parts of Central Park, where they bloom profusely on hillsides. Other highlights include carefully tended beds of tulips, a reminder of the city's Dutch origins. *New York, New York.*

OPPOSITE: Frederick Law Olmstead and Calvert Vaux created a masterpiece of landscape design with New York's Central Park. Groves of trees, expansive lawns, and flowery byways are accented by such features as Belvedere Castle which sits atop a steep hill. *New York, New York.*

FOLLOWING PAGE: The combination of shrubs, flowering blossoms, and water gently flowing from a fountain provides beauty for the eye and relaxation for the spirit. These are elements that have been exploited, in countless variations, throughout the history of American garden design, on the largest estates and in the smallest private plots. *Kennett Square, Pennsylvania.*

LEFT: **Longwood Gardens consists of 1,050 acres of landscaped gardens, fine glass conservatories, and stretches of meadows and woodlands. The Main Conservatory, shown here, is one of its chief attractions. *Kennett Square, Pennsylvania.***

LEFT: **Acting as a museum of the history of gardening and American gardening in particular, Longwood Gardens contains over 11, 000 different types of plants, on display year round. Though spring and summer are the most spectacular, there is an abundance of botanical wonders in the other seasons as well. *Kennett Square, Pennsylvania.***

OPPOSITE: **Many of America's finest public gardens were once planned, maintained, and held by wealthy owners. Beginning in 1906, Pierre S DuPont launched the development of Longwood Gardens on his immense private estate. Carefully expanded over the years, it was opened to the public upon DuPont's death in 1954. *Kennett Square, Pennsylvania,***

RIGHT: **The Topiary Garden at Longwood is a principal attraction. Though by its difficulty beyond the reach of most gardeners, it is, nevertheless, a continuing source of fascination. Here we see a whimsical teapot straight from the pages of *Alice in Wonderland. Kennett Square, Pennsylvania.***

OPPOSITE: **Topiary is a sculptural technique developed to enhance the European formal gardens of centuries past. Beginning with the clipping of shrubs into simple geometric shapes, it soon advanced to more itricate designs to represent animals, birds, or nymphs. The most commonly used plants for this form are arborvitae, box, privet, and yew. *Kennett Square, Pennsylvania.***

FLOWER GARDENS AND GARDEN DESIGN

Flower gardens marked a return to formality, especially in the small garden, but the plants in it were often the latest arrivals from Africa or South America. Clipper ships guaranteed fast transport, and they arrived with wisteria, bleeding hearts, fuchsias, dahlias, gloxinias, cannas, red salvia, petunias, lobelias, and geraniums.

These plants with their vivid blossoms, and coleuses with their patterned leaves were among the favorites in carpet-bedded gardens. In the small gardens of modest homes, this might only have been a circular bed in the center of a front lawn, or a centerpiece in a circular drive.

Seed companies responded to public demand and produced new varieties of plants with longer flowering seasons. The names of these varieties, such as Burpee's "Defiance" pansies and petunias also advertised the plant's ability to "defy nature" and bloom more than the ordinary pansy or petunia.

THE HOME HORTICULTURAL GARDEN

Plants could now be chosen for their hardiness as well as their beauty. The ready availability of glass enhanced the popularity of greenhouses and conservatories. This interest in plants created the home horticultural garden. Gardeners' interest in plants, and knowledge of the conditions in which they best thrived applied science to beauty, and gardeners soon became interested in the combinations of plants that would lend their garden a succession of buds and blooms throughout the year.

This was called the mingled flower garden, and was typically arranged so that the showiest plants were repeated in different parts of the garden. Furthermore, the plants in the flower beds were graduated in size with the smallest flowers nearest the front, the taller flowers behind them, and the tallest of all at the back.

WESTWARD HO!

When Lewis and Clark returned from their exploration of the northwest in 1806, they had mapped a mountain range and a vast desert, insuperable objects to westward expansion. Later in the century, better transportation by land and over rivers encouraged westward immigration. Those who traveled west were those whose "restlessness and disposition to change," Andrew Jackson Downing believed, could be rehabilitated by a peaceful garden. Religious sects who hoped emulate the success of the Quakers, emigrated west to establish their own peaceful gardens and Utopian communities.

CHAPTER THREE

THE PLAINS, THE ROCKIES, AND THE FAR WEST

The American West was a place of pristine beauty. Breathless descriptions of its natural wonders by travelers continued to draw the curious and the hopeful westward. Many observers marveled at North America's vastness and natural beauty, but were appalled by the crudeness of the new prairie and pioneer settlements. One referred to them as "God-forsaken and God-forgotten."

These early visitors would not recognize the city of fountains and wide boulevards that Kansas City, Missouri has become. Denver, a former gold-mining community, is now home to Botanic Gardens with acres of alpine plants. Santa Fe is synonymous with a distinct style of clean lines and bold colors—a mixture of Spanish and Native American art and design.

ARBOR DAY

Johnny Appleseed and Colonel Marie Joseph Lafayette were the first individuals who assiduously planted trees and attempted to forest the Midwest with orchards and ornamental shade trees. Nineteenth-century immigrants to Kansas, who traveled there from New England, astounded their neighbors from other parts of the country by growing ornamental and fruit trees with great success on the prairie.

Tree planting became an encouraged ritual in new communities. The idea of "Arbor Day" a day reserved for tree planting, belongs to Julius Sterling Morton. Morton lived in New York and then in Michigan, before settling in Nebraska in 1859, where he became one of the state's first senators.

Morton planted a large apple orchard outside of Nebraska City, and sponsored a day for civic tree planting. In 1872, at his urging, the state legislature officially set aside a day for this purpose, to be observed annually. From Nebraska, the idea spread to other states and into Canada. Morton's Nebraska estate, greenhouse, and arboretum have been preserved as a state historical park called Arbor Lodge.

BELOW: A bed of woodbine accented by bright orange berries grows before the historic Surveyor General's Office in Santa Fe. Today the city is a unique garden spot, as it has been throughout its history. _Santa Fe, New Mexico._

PRIDE OF PLACE

Nineteenth-century pioneers found fertile ground as far north as the Red River Valley in the Dakotas, and in Kansas, Nebraska, and Iowa, too. The change in climate and soil meant that the trees and plants of New England did not always thrive in the severe winters of the North, or in the arid stretches of the Southwest. Nevertheless, settlers were determined to turn it into a garden wherever they could.

France had explored the Mississippi north to Detroit, and French Canadians were the first to

OPPOSITE: This lush, refreshing scene can be found in the central garden of the old Spanish Governor's House in San Antonio. Shady and cooling refuges such as this were a necessity in the hot climate of the West. _San Antonio, Texas._

BELOW: **In the late eighteenth century oriental rose species were introduced to the West and eventually found their way to the Americas. Aside from their astonishing beauty, one of their novelties was that some put forth yellow blooms. Today, of course, after yaers of hybridization, a full palette of colors is available. *Jefferson County, Ohio.***

settle the Midwestern states, and, wherever possible, to plant orchards. When transportation, both on land and by water, improved in the nineteenth century, so did commerce. The population and wealth of the river cities on the large tributaries to the Mississippi increased. Towns like Evansville, Illinois, New Albany, Indiana, and Madison, Wisconsin, sprang up on the shores of the Ohio River. There, residents built impressive homes and gardens. By 1850, Cincinnati was the horticultural center of the Ohio Valley, and almost all the region.

Chicago, in 1860, was considered a city of gardens, only thirty years after its initial settlement. Then called "The Garden City," Chicago's summer and winter gardens, where one could dine surrounded by ornamental plants, were known throughout the Midwest.

Clergyman, Henry Ward Beecher made Indianapolis the center for horticulture in Indiana. In his abundant garden, there were many flowering shrubs, fruiting plants and trees, and his "especial favorite," the rose.

ROSE GARDENS

Henry Ward Beecher's enthusiasm for the rose was almost universal among American gardeners. By the middle of the nineteenth century, rose collecting became increasingly popular in gardens throughout the United States. The intensive cultivation of the rose is one of the notable points of nineteenth century garden history.

BELOW: **Perhaps no other flower is more beloved by Americans than the rose. It's popularity has been widespread in the United States since the earliest times. Of all the many rose types, the climping rose is one of the most decorative, with its ability to grow in masses on buildings and trellises. *Kennett Square, Pennsylvania.***

LEFT: **Roses grow in the wild in northern temperate latitudes worldwide, and have been thriving for at least thirty million years. Wild roses, such as these growing in a Texas field, were an all-important element in early Western gardens. *Harris County, Texas.***

New species appeared in rapid succession. The hardy hybrid-perpetuals, which were the most popular rose in America throughout the nineteenth century, were known as the "Remontant" roses.

The explosion in varieties and longer flowering seasons made roses the most popular garden shrub, and they became the favorite plants for creating scented arbors and pergolas, particularly in the South. Roses were used as the focal point of many gardens, and were often grouped in gardens that excluded all other plants. They were planted in informal groupings, but many rose gardens, especially those of the well-to-do, harkened back to the geometric beds and straight paths of the formal garden.

RIGHT: **This interesting, abstract display combines masses of white tufty iberis surrounding a grouping of white-star flowers. In the background, a free-form espalier design grows on a wooden garden fence.** ***San Francisco, California.***

BELOW: **Wild roses, or species roses, are ideal garden plants because they are extremely hardy and require little care. With their simple, five-petaled flowers, they provide colorful displays when planted in groups, as seen in this array of blooms at the New York Botanical Garden.** ***New York, New York.***

LEFT: This front garden is crafted of local rocks and boulders with plantings of drought-resistant shrubs and ground covers. The shrubs are trimmed in the topiary-style, but their irregular form strikes a more modern note, and appears to replicate, in greenery, the shapes of the rocks. *San Jose, California.*

LEFT: Taking a cue from nature, Western gardeners have experimented with a variety of rock gardens to artfully copy the mixture of form and texture created by plants and stones in the wild. Plots like this private garden are prized for their beauty and easy maintenance. *San Jose, California.*

ABOVE: **The main facade of the Mission Santa Barbara, dating from 1786, is seen here with a grouping of indigenous plants in the foreground. Various cactus species and low-growing succulents create a display of contrasting foliage that springs naturally from the landscape. *Santa Barbara, California.***

MISSION GARDENS

Franciscan Missionaries settled the West Coast and the Southwest. Their presence was sparse north of San Francisco, and Mission Santa Rosa. The missions they built were planted with oranges, figs, olives and grapes. These were cultivated only around the mission community itself. Some of the flowers they featured included the Castillian rose—brought to California from Mexico— sweet-peas, hollyhocks, nasturtiums, and white lilies.

The first mission established in Alta California was in San Diego in 1769 by Junipero Serra. For nearly fifty years, the Spanish were the main European settlers, handing out large land grants to families. However, shortly after Mexico declared its of independence from Spain in 1821, the missions fell into decline.

In the 1880s, a revival of interest in Spanish colonial gardens developed, resulting in the restoration of the mission gardens. San Juan Capistrano and its gardens were among the first to be renovated, using traditional materials such as adobe. Almost all the California missions along the El Camino Real from San Diego to San Francisco have now been restored, along with their churchyards, fountains, and patios, and can be visited today.

RIGHT: **San Diego's Presidio is a fortress that once protected the local mission from Indian attack. The gardens of such missions were created by priests and monks who imported a number of flowering plants to the region. This mass of modern blooms before the Presidio reflects this tradition. *San Diego, California,***

LEFT: Like its counterparts in other regions of the country, the main conservatory of San Francisco's Golden Gate Park, offers instruction not only on local plants but on species from around the world. *San Francisco, California.*

BELOW: Trellises, fences, and other architectural elements have long been incorporated into garden design. The "follies" of the eighteenth century and the gazebos and garden houses of the ninetenth are recalled in this modern yet traditional structure. *San Diego, California.*

COLONIAL GARDENS OF THE SOUTHWEST

Founded in 1605, Santa Fe, New Mexico retains much of its Spanish colonial flavor. Now as then, the city is known for its many interior courtyard gardens surrounded by simple, low houses. Each courtyard is a small green oasis planted with trees, shrubs, and vines, arranged around a central pool or well. The contrast between these lush havens and the stark, arid countryside is astonishing.

The heart of Santa Fe is still the Spanish style plaza, and the city has preserved the San Miguel Mission, originally built in 1625 by the Tlaxcala Indians. Spanish colonial gardens can be found elsewhere in the Southwest. Taos, New Mexico is a small, graceful city full of courtyards and walled Spanish-style enclosures, shaded by elms and cottonwood trees. The fortress of Tucson, Arizona's presidio district dates back to 1776, and is another example of the Spanish influence.

LEFT: A hand-carved wooden statue of St. Francis, created by a local craftsman, is the focal point of a quiet corner of the chapel garden of the Bishop's Lodge in Santa Fe. The use of local artworks to embellish homes, churches, and public places has preserved and encouraged appreciation of the region's folk art. *Santa Fe, New Mexico.*

LEFT: Here is an exterior view of the lovely enclosed gardens of the Inn on the Almeda in Santa Fe. A mixture of clinging ivy, tall evergreens, ground-clinging flowers, and low-growing shrubs has created a modern-day oasis. *Santa Fe, New Mexico.*

FOLLOWING PAGE: Butchart Gardens is one of the most spectacular horticultural sites in the Pacific Northwest. Here, the gardening aspirations of both Canada and the United States are celebrated, showing what can be achieved in this lush, plant-friendly region. *Victoria, British Columbia.*

OPPOSITE: Pansies, tulips, and Calendula cinfraria are but a few of the many different flowers clustered around a small rock outcropping. Influenced by oriental design, modern gardeners incorporate these "impediments" into their garden instead of clearing them away. *Berkeley, California.*

RIGHT: **Beatrix Farrand, the creator of the gardens at Dumbarton Oaks, also provided the designs for the Fioli Estate. Influenced by such English gardeners as Gertrude Jekyll, she was sensitive to the importance of color. Here, masses of wallflowers and tulips contrast to the green of the lawn and the formal fountain in the background. *Fioli Estate, California.***

RIGHT: **This garden close-up is an example the blending of colors, shapes, and textures that many gardeners have long strived to achieve. Here, low plantings of marigolds, petunias, and Celosivae are separated by a stone retaining wall from a display of white roses. *Bonneville, Oregon.***

OPPOSITE: **Here, nature's way of plant survival is cleverly adapted to garden design with this artful distribution of purple lobelia along a crannied stone wall. More severe that some rock gardens, this plan suggests the hardiness of alpine flowers in the wild. *San Juan Island, Washington.***

NEW GARDENS OF GRAND HOUSES

By the end of the nineteenth century, nearly every town had its avenues of grand houses. Estates were established in relatively recently settled regions such as Oregon's Willamette Valley, where the Hoover-Minthurne House in the pioneer town of Newburg is located. Portland's Pittock Mansion is also one of these estates.

The majority of nineteenth century gardeners applied themselves to garden design in the same way they decorated their houses, often with a fussy attention to detail. Flower gardeners of the nineteenth century abhorred a vacuum. Ornamentation with mass produced benches, chairs, basins, cupids, and urns sometimes bordered on the excessive.

One garden historian attributed the eclectic influences upon American garden design, not to the variations in climate and geography, but to the fact that America lacked an "indigenous, national gardening tradition."

Through the end of the nineteenth century, each successive wave of immigration brought people with knowledge and memories of their childhood gardens and homes. Those who later became well-to-do imported the gardens—and sometimes the houses—of Europe's aristocracy to their American estates. Their architects and gardeners did not always immediately find a way of adapting old gardens to new surroundings. That would take the efforts of several visionary landscape designers.

CHAPTER FOUR

DEVELOPING AN AMERICAN STYLE

Classical architecture had long appealed to Americans, as can be seen from the buildings that survive from the colonial and Federal periods. However, the classical influence in garden design had yet to be articulated in the American back yard.

American gardeners and designers had looked to the landscape gardens of England and the formal gardens of France for models. These garden styles were inspired by classical gardens, but had been translated to suit each country and climate. Furthermore, the classical garden had been further modified to please the lavish tastes of monarchs and aristocrats.

THE CLASSICAL GARDEN IN AMERICA

By the close of the nineteenth century, sophisticated Americans were growing weary of the Victorian fondness for sentimentality in house and garden design. A young American art student, Charles Platt, echoed this feeling in his 1894 book, *Italian Gardens*. Based on his study of surviving Renaissance and Baroque gardens in Italy, Platt's book offered an elegant alternative to the eclectic chaos that had come to dominate the nineteenth-century flower garden. It also led to his first design commission and to a career that would be instrumental in shaping the profession of landscape architecture.

RIGHT: Early in the twentieth century American designers found inspiration in the famed gardens created in Renaissaance Italy, such as the Boboli Gardens in Florence. A highlight of this spot is the moated garden known as Islotto, with its renowned statuary and pots of fragrant lemon and orange trees. *Florence, Italy*

OPPOSITE: The gardens of Agecroft Hall were designed to match the house itself, a fifteenth-century half-timbered manor house from Lancashire, England that was taken apart in the 1920s and reassembled in America. *Richmond, Virginia.*

BELOW: **The secret garden, located below the ground level of the Villa Vizcaya and the terraces of the main garden, is just one of the surprises prepared for visitors. Others include a warterside gazebo and an outdoor casino. *Miami, Florida.***

In 1904, the novelist Edith Wharton joined forces with Platt, with the publication of her book, *Italian Villas and Their Gardens* . In it, she attempted to define a path out of what she perceived was the confusion in American garden design. Wharton believed that rules of good design could be drawn from the Renaissance gardens of Italy. She presented each Italian garden in her book, as a "prolongation of the house."

In Wharton's estimation, the best kind of garden consisted of a series of enclosed spaces or "rooms," rather than a single spacious expanse of unbounded terrain. Though she conceived of the garden as a cluster of rooms that provided a gradual retreat from the house into nature, she was distressed by the interior decorator's approach to garden design, and she was critical of the popularity and dominance of flowers in the American garden. "Adventurous effects" such as vivid floral displays had no place in the classical garden. "The Italian garden does not exist for its flowers; its flowers exist for it..."

Italian Villas drew upon source material from books in four languages dating back to the seventeenth century. It combined firsthand experience with garden history, and included brief biographical profiles of sixty notable and important garden architects. Almost forty villa gardens were examined, many by means of garden sketches and illustrations.

Edith Wharton set the style for gardeners and garden lovers of discrimination. Many followed her lead, and many more digressed from it. One of the finest interpretations of a sixteenth century Italian garden was created between 1912 and 1916 at the Villa Vizcaya near Miami, Florida. The Vizcaya gardens capture the "inherent beauty" of the Italian garden, which Mrs. Wharton believed was the balanced grouping of all the parts, of light and shade, water and pavement, terrace and lawn. At Vizcaya, flowers flourish in Florida's tropical climate among the other essential elements of the Italian garden, "marble, water, and perennial verdure."

BELOW: **Designer Paul Chalfin declared that at Vizcaya he had created something up to now unachieved in the New World...a house and garden that date from a proud and vigorous past. *Miami, Florida.***

RIGHT: **Offering a variety of moods, classical garden sculpture often mixes stately grandeur with moments of whimsy. This charming sculptural detail gives Vizcaya's Frog Fountain its name.** ***Miami, Florida.***

RIGHT: **Inspired by Italian designs, the gardens of Vizcaya incorporate sculpture, fountains, and architectural elements to create an array of expansive vistas and charming walkways.** ***Miami, Florida.***

OPPOSITE: **The main entrance to Vizcaya, a Venetian-style villa built between 1914 and 1922 by multimillionaire James Deering. The extensive gardens were based on Italian models and were influenced by Edith Wharton's theories of garden design.** ***Miami, Florida.***

LEFT: **In the 1920s, the American landscape designer, Beatrix Farrand laid out a ten-acre formal garden for the grounds of the historic mansion, Dumbarton Oaks. Apart from creating spectacular displays like these herbaceous borders, she also incorporated such preexisting elements as an orangery dating from 1810. *Washington,, D. C.***

LEFT: **The intricate design and baroque flair of the Pebble Garden at Dumbarton Oaks could easily be mistaken as part of the grounds of a French chateau or an Italian villa. *Washington, D. C.***

OPPOSITE: **Freely adapting European ideas to American needs, such features as the dual staircase in the terrace gardens of Dumbarton Oaks were created. *Washington, D. C.***

Edith Wharton's niece, Beatrix Farrand, became a landscape architect of note. She designed the landscape gardens of many fine homes, including the Filoli estate near San Francisco, but her best known garden is the one she designed at Dumbarton Oaks outside of Washington, D.C.

Dumbarton Oaks is a celebrated and much-visited example of a free interpretation of the Italian garden. It was designed by Farrand between 1921 and 1947, and answers Edith Wharton's call to grasp the Italian garden's "underlying spirit." However, the use of flowers and woodland at

RIGHT: The restored garden of the colonial-period Glebe House is the work of twentieth-century English landscape designer Gertrude Jekyll. Noted for her painterly, impressionistic use of color, she was a major influence on American designer, Beatrix Farrand. This is one of only two Jekyll gardens in the United States. *Woodbury, Connecticut.*

BELOW: Within the formal gardens of the Vanderbilt Estate can be found this enclosed area with its classical statuary and reflecting pool, epitomizing the opulence of The Gilded Age. *Hyde Park, New York.*

Dumbarton Oaks is clearly inspired by the work of contemporary English garden designers, whose work Farrand admired.

The formal restraint of the classical Italian garden, though beautiful, was not entirely at one with the opulent spirit of the Gilded Age. Nevertheless, from the end of the nineteenth century and into the second decade of the twentieth, classical gardens were created throughout the United States.

GARDENS OF THE GILDED AGE

The proliferation of parvenu fortunes in America in the late nineteenth and early twentieth centuries was immediately succeeded by the creation of new country estates and extensive gardens in and around almost every American city. The newly wealthy often had more than one estate. For example, the Vanderbilts had country estates in Newport, Rhode Island and on Jekyll Island off the coast of Georgia—and so did their friends.

Formal gardens surrounded most of these impressive new homes. Often the larger the fortune, the larger the garden. Many, like Huntington House in California, have been preserved as botanical gardens. Others are open to the public as state parks or simply as historic gardens like that of Longwood—of an earlier age—in Pennsylvannia's Brandywine Valley.

These gardens with their outdoor rooms, were not so much a compliment to the interior rooms of the house, as they were stage sets for costume balls, Easter egg and treasure hunts, and outdoor theme parties. Gardens could be dressed up just like the guests, and they were. Usually, the garden was made so remarkable that guests could be immediately transported by the setting to another place or era. Reminders of ancient civilizations, such as marble statues and avenues of palms or cypresses enhanced this effect, and made the gardens the perfect settings for romantic trysts, noisy festivities, and, at times, high drama.

ABOVE: Beautiful sculpture and other artworks from around the world were combined with carefully selected trees and shrubs to create the sumptuous pleasure gardens surrounding Hearst Castle, built during the 1920s and 1930s by the famous newspaper tycoon, William Randolph Hearst. _San Simeon, California._

William Randolph Hearst's country estate at San Simeon had just such a garden. Hearst was the wealthy newspaper baron and publishing tycoon. He was an avid collector, and the main house at San Simeon, Casa Grande, was decorated with his acquisitions. The baroque water garden, a large mosaic pool, is at the bottom of a cascade of steps and terraces. The pool itself is graced by an authentic classical temple, while a few evergreens lend the grounds the "perennial verdure" of the classical garden. Evening parties were lit by illuminated globes atop identical classical statues on successive terraces. The effect at night, with the water reflected in the brilliant blue pool, must have been

ghostly and grand. Reveling in this garden with its hilltop location, guests could easily have felt they were on the roof of the world.

The stock market crash of 1929 ruined many fortunes, and reduced many others. The introduction of income tax curtailed lavish spending. Marriages foundered, and couples separated. Unoccupied, expensive to maintain, and difficult to sell, some estates and their gardens simply fell into ruin. Others were sold or entrusted to state or charitable institutions in the hope that the gardens would be maintained, and many have become city botanical gardens and historical sites.

LEFT: **In the South Belvedere garden of Orton Plantation we see a mixture of design influences, from the formal to the naturalistic. Note the contrast between the formal flower beds, surrounded by low hedge borders, to the lush, almost untamed, quality of the massive display of azaleas blooming in the background. *Winnabow, North Carolina.***

REGIONAL ARCHITECTURE AND GARDEN STYLES

In the early 1920s, several factors were at work on American garden style. None of them were new, but all were pervasive. The first was the style of the classical garden, and classical architecture. The other influence was the arts and crafts movement. Primarily a British movement, begun by William Morris in the latter half of the nineteenth century, its aim was to enhance the status of the artisan and the decorative arts. It was anti-industrial, and urged a return to the "goodness" of regional handicrafts and simple decoration. It advocated a revival of local traditions in style, material, and workmanship, and helped to encourage the recreation of simple gardens of the previous era, and the large scale restoration of others.

In the 1920s, Virginia architect, William Lawrence Bottomley helped to perpetuate the living tradition of the Southern plantation garden. He revived an old form and recreated it without the historic restraints applied to garden designers doing actual restorations, like those at Williamsburg. Bottomley felt he was creating estates and villas that were purely American in

FOLLOWING PAGE: **Known as a torii in Japan, the red structure shown here is the focal point of an artificial lake at the Brooklyn Botanic Garden. These simple yet elegant gateways are traditionally used as symbolic portals to Shinto temples. *Brooklyn, New York.***

RIGHT: **In the 1920s, the Southern ghost garden emerged. Meant to be enjoyed mostly at night under the light of a full moon, its most important elements were white blooms and gray Spanish moss hanging from the limbs of massive trees. *Winnabow, North Cariolina.***

OPPOSITE: **The fashion for European design in the early twentieth century was not expressed by imitation alone. Virginia House—once a tudor English priory—was imported, like its neighbor, Agecroft Hall, piece by piece to be reconstructed as a private residence. Care was taken to be sure the grounds complemented the character of the dwelling. *Richmond, Virginia.***

大明神

ABOVE: **In the Japanese garden, the incorporation of rocks and sand into the design scheme is as important as the disposition of plants. Structures, such as this graceful bridge and heavy stone lantern, are also integrated. These particular examples are found at the Brooklyn Botanic Garden.** ***Brooklyn, New York.***

style, but the larger question of the American garden had yet to be addressed.

That question was man's relationship to the landscape. For some time, landscape architects had been postulating a garden style that demonstrated a unity between house and garden. This was a concept that Frank Lloyd Wriight, the architectural Emerson of the prairies, embraced whole heartedly. Wright believed that nature itself held poetic inspiration, the starting point from which to build the house and design a garden. The houses he designed, such as Fallingwater in western Pennsylvania, and his own home, Taliesin West, near Scottsdale Arizona, marry architecture to the landscape.Wright's belief in man's organic relationship to his environment was formed by his fondness for the Wisconsin farmland where he spent his boyhood, and by his absorption of the principles of Japanese architecture and design. The cult of nature is at the core of Japanese life and art, and Japanese architecture strives to unify the house with its natural surroundings.

EAST MEETS WEST

Man Japanese principles and traditions actually had their origins in China. China, like North America, is a country with dramatic and dramatically various topography. Botanists have explored its richly varied regions to discover plants and flowers. Orchids, chrysanthemums, tree peonies, roses, and lotuses are only a few of the horticultural treasures brought back from the East. In China, as much as possible, all the natural beauty of the country was incorporated into the garden. Imperial gardens were immense, but in small gardens, stones served as mountains, and ponds as lakes.

Chinese garden design is based upon the philosophy of the Dao. Briefly, the ruling principle of the Dao is "the way." The Dao—being total abstraction and essence—defies definition, but those who have studied it say, "The Dao makes things what they are, but it is not itself a thing. Nothing can produce Dao, yet everything has Dao within it." Gardening in accordance with the Dao puts the gardener in an intimate connection with all the elements of nature.

The art of garden planning is like the Chinese art of feng shui. Chinese garden design is an artful arrangement of the rough and soft elements, found in stones and water: An arrangement that captures the essential forces of nature. A garden that contains the fundamental elements is in perfect accordance with the nature itself. A stroll down the path of such a garden, or a few moments spent sitting in it, can bring the individual into a grace-like state of communion with the natural world.

This description of the Dao is a woefully simple reduction, and only proves how elusive "the way" can be when forced into a single definition. However, gardeners everywhere whose gardens provide them with a sublime connection with the changing seasons, and who strive to work in accordance with nature, will have no trouble understanding the elusive principles of "the way."

Garden design in accordance with the Dao gives the impression of fluidity. This element can be called "flow," and it is present in the Japanese garden, which influenced the thinking of Frank Lloyd Wright. The Japanese garden, though originally based on the same principle, is an extremely formal one.

JAPANESE GARDENS

Traditionally, no house in Japan is considered complete without a surrounding garden. The opened-sided architecture of traditional Japanese homes—which Frank Lloyd Wright imitated and improvised upon—minimizes the boundaries between house and garden. The use of sliding screens opens the house to the outdoors, and the transparency of the traditional rice screen silhouettes the garden's foliage, transforming it into a changeable ink drawing.

It is not surprising that Zen Buddhism has influenced the art of garden design in a country where communion with nature is uplifting and conducive to contemplation. Trees, stones, sand, moss, and water are the basic elements of garden design. They are superficially monotonous to those who love abundant displays of flowers, but in the hands of an artist, infinitely elaborate.

ABOVE: Bellingrath Gardens, today open to the public, is the result of the life's work of Walter and Bessie Bellingrath. who created over sixty-five acres of variously planted areas in pursuit of their horticultural passions. The high, arching bridge seen here is the highlight of the Japanese garden the couple created. *Mobile, Alabama*

LEFT: A gound-hugging bonsai azalea in full bloom graces the Japanese garden at the Brooklyn Botanic Garden. *Brooklyn, New York.*

Four distinctly different styles of gardens developed from the Zen aesthetic. Of these, the three gardens, most familiar to westerners, are the dry rock garden, the water garden, and the tea garden. This last type is recreated in botanical gardens throughout the United States.

Gardens of the east often recreate the landscape in miniature. In Japanese rock and sand gardens, mountains are created out of symmetrical mounds of sand. Waterfalls and streams are suggested by flowing lines raked into the sand. Shrubs may be shaped into round green boulders. Azaleas shaped in such a fashion provide surprising bursts of flame when in bloom.Whatever the variations, Japanese gardens are created as places of contemplation and rest.

ABOVE: **One of America's great urban garden spots is Lombard Street in San Francisco, with its steep, flower-lined curves. Though such masses of blooms can be found in many other places, this landscaping concept seems to capture the spirit of this unique city.** ***San Francisco, California.***

MODERNISM IN THE AMERICAN GARDEN

The abstractions of modern art and sculpture have also influenced garden design. Unde, such as the yucca and agave, with new eyes. Some began using them in isolation for their form alone. Light itself, especially the strong sunlight characteristic of the desert and sections of the Pacific coast, offered garden designers a chance to create dramatic vertical and horizontal lines of shadow in spare gardens of gravel, grass, and concrete that showcase an architectural plant.

These courtyard gardens are too austere for some, but like Wright's houses, they take their inspiration from the surrounding landscape. They also, more often than not, conserve water. At the end of the twentieth century, those with true feeling for the natural world now seek conservation of all kinds.

We live with the worrying knowledge that our natural resources are finite, and we wish to preserve our wild landscapes as much as possible. This awareness cannot but help shape our relationship to our environment, just as it has helped to shape the idea of the natural habitat garden.

THE NATURAL HABITAT GARDEN

The natural habitat garden is a concept that is unique and uniquely suited to the gardens and varied regions of the United States. It requires a knowledge of the countryside, combined with a feel for gardening. It is not feng shui, but it is a "way" that invites nature to provide the rules for the design of the garden. The natural habitat garden takes a giant step back from the historical idea—in the western world—of the garden as a creation superior to the surrounding landscape.

The natural habitat garden proposes a way through or to the wilderness, for those with problem plots of land, or for those who would like to reintroduce native grasses and plants to existing gardens. Contemporary landscape architects are combining conservation with contemporary design, and allowing nature to extemporize. To do this, gardeners do not attempt to change the land, but to design to its requirements. In the process, gardeners can produce their own small nature reserves.

Some gardeners have interpreted the natural habitat garden as simply the survival of the fittest. Others are taking the opportunity to reintroduce prairie steppes and wildflower gardens. Those who are dedicated to wild gardening believe it

OPPOSITE: **The possibility of Eden regained is suggested by the conceit of placing the standing figures of Adam and Eve in an idyllic forest setting. Such touches remind us that gardens are places for comtemplation, reflection, and fantasy.** ***Monkton, Maryland.***

RIGHT: **Here we see the house and spectacular terraces of the Ladew Topiary Gardens. Note that though the sizes of the three parallel rows differ, the proportion of their shapes is perfectly maintained. *Monkton, Maryland.***

should be more than a passing fashion. Other gardeners have taken the dictum of the natural habitat garden to create a cascading display of alpine flowers growing on the rocks of a steep and stony garden.

SMALL GARDENS

Even the smallest garden provides an opportunity to commune with nature. They are valuable places of refuge and repose. Plants take on an even greater importance in the small garden. Herb gardens and flower gardens are uniquely suited to small spaces. Even a vertical space offers the opportunity to create a hanging garden.

Gardens are as individual as the people who create them, and plants should be chosen and gardens designed to afford the maximum pleasure. A hedge of old garden roses with honeysuckle and a climbing vine, will impart luscious scent, beautiful blossoms, and a hint of romantic wildness.

BELOW: **The sculpture garden at Ladew is a topiary gallery, displaying a variety of froms, including birds. *Monkton, Maryland.***

Color can lift the spirits or sooth them, and vegetables, herbs, and flowers, whether grown in containers on a terrace or in a long fertile bed, allow gardeners to bring the outdoors inside.

Gardening is an art like no other. It uses living materials and requires the gardener to imagine how they will grow. It is discouraging when plants die, and disheartening when shrubs or flowers are destroyed by strong winds, an unseasonal frost, or an energetic puppy. Nevertheless, most would agree with Francis Bacon that gardening "is the greatest refreshment of the spirits of man."

Gardening also requires the gardener to be mindful of the small things. The beauty of a single blossom, or rain inside the petal, can stay a gardeners hand, or still a heart. Certainly, being mindful of the small things is one of the most ethical ways to live.

A PURELY AMERICAN GARDEN

An American garden can be largely what you make it, whether it is a flowering pot on a terrace, a garden of stones and trickling water, an avenue of flowering crab apples, a hillside alpine garden, or a garden for boggy ground.

Gardens everywhere are living affirmation that the seasons pass and life goes on. In this way, gardens make themselves more than a quiet refuge or a safe place for children to play. Gardens become a place of comfort and companionship. Gardening itself, despite the practical hard work, keeps gardeners not very far from wonder, and makes gardening a process that is as mysterious as the spring leaf or blossom on a dry twig. The American garden, like North America to the first botanical explorers, is a place of discovery.

OPPOSITE: **Parallel to an interest in European design, a desire to revisit the perceived glamour and romace of the Old South developed. Surviving Southern plantation houses, with their classical architecture and evocative landscaped grounds became quite popular during the 1920s. *Orton Plantation, Winnabow, North Carolina.***

INDEX

Page numbers in **bold-face** type indicate photo captions.